The LORD bless you
and keep you;
the LORD make his face shine on you
and be gracious to you;
the LORD turn his face towards you
and give you peace.

NUMBERS 6:24-26 NIV

Hear, LORD, when I cry with my voice,
And be gracious to me and answer me.

PSALM 27:7 NASB

_____

_____

_____

_____

_____

_____

_____

Hymn writer Edward Joy saw in worry an opportunity—an opportunity to understand our weakness and celebrate our God's strength. An opportunity to find rest and peace in the God who is greater than our needs and better than we sometimes think. Joy wrote:

> Is there a heart o'erbound by sorrow?
> Is there a life weighed down by care?
> Come to the cross, each burden bearing;
> All your anxiety—leave it there.

> No other friend so swift to help you,
> No other friend so quick to hear,
> No other place to leave your burden,
> No other one to hear your prayer.

> All your anxiety, all your care,
> Bring to the mercy seat, leave it there,
> Never a burden He cannot bear,
> Never a friend like Jesus!

FROM *WISDOM FOR OUR WORRIES* BY BILL CROWDER

Patience is waiting—peacefully, quietly, expectantly—on those we love: God and others. Patience can't be bought. It has to be cultivated, one circumstance at a time.

FROM *DWELL* BY SANDRA BYRD

_____

_____

_____

_____

_____

_____

_____

_____

_____

_____

_____

_____

_____

_____

_____

_____

_____

_____

_____

_____

Walk in a manner worthy of the calling with which you
have been called, with all humility and gentleness, with
patience, bearing with one another in love, being diligent
to keep the unity of the Spirit in the bond of peace.

EPHESIANS 4:1–3 NASB

Father God, I need you. When the world around me spins out of control, I need you. When the people I love are at odds with each other, I need you. When I fear for the future and grieve over the past, I need you. Help me lift my eyes to you and remember that you are Lord over all. Nothing escapes your sight, and nothing is too hard for you. Surround me with peace and grow my trust. Help me rest in your mercy. In the strong name of Jesus I ask, amen.

FROM *REFRESH YOUR HOPE* BY LORI HATCHER

I will listen to what God the LORD says;
he promises peace to his people.

PSALM 85:8 NIV

Long before self-help books dominated Amazon, God offered to help us live our best lives. He still does. One where we can overcome obstacles, find peace in the midst of chaos, experience joy, understand what it feels like to be truly loved, and do amazing things He's already equipped us to do. It's way better than self-help could ever be. God's offer can restore our souls.

FROM *RESTORE MY SOUL* BY LAURA L. SMITH

I am leaving you with a gift—peace of mind and heart. And the peace
I give is a gift the world cannot give. So don't be troubled or afraid.

JOHN 14:27 NLT

We long for peace, Lord! Help us to know how to be peacemakers in our bitterly divided world. We call on you to give us wisdom. Guide us by your Spirit so that we will turn away from all that displeases you.

We call on you to help us, Lord, as we try to live for you in our challenges. Show us your ways to your peace . . . and thank you for your many blessings.

FROM *FREEDOM FROM MY FEARS* BY HAROLD MYRA

_____

_____

_____

_____

_____

_____

_____

_____

_____

_____

_____

THANK GOD FOR TODAY'S BLESSINGS

-
-
-
-
-
-

Genesis reveals that when human beings live with God, they are able to live at peace and in harmony with other human beings. One of the most beautiful stories in this book is that of Abraham's dwelling under the oaks of Mamre in a place surrounded by Canaanites, a people that for many years had been his enemy. But God worked in the life of Abraham so that even his enemies were at peace with him. . . .

Genesis declares that only human beings in fellowship with God can know supreme happiness—the righteousness, peace, and joy we always hunger for. This realisation comes only as people discover that the indwelling God is the answer to all their needs.

FROM *ADVENTURING THROUGH THE BIBLE*, HOME EDITION,

BY RAY C. STEDMAN

If possible, so far as it depends on you, live peaceably with all.

ROMANS 12:18 ESV

_____

_____

_____

_____

_____

_____

_____

_____

_____

_____

_____

_____

_____

_____

_____

_____

_____

_____

_____

You will keep in perfect peace
those whose minds are steadfast,
because they trust in you.
Trust in the LORD forever,
for the LORD, the LORD himself, is the Rock eternal.

ISAIAH 26:3-4 NIV

_____

_____

_____

_____

_____

_____

_____

_____

_____

_____

_____

_____

_____

_____

_____

_____

_____

_____

In peace I will lie down and sleep, for you
alone, O LORD, will keep me safe.

PSALM 4:8 NLT

Do not be anxious about anything, but in every situation, by prayer and petition, with thanksgiving, present your requests to God. And the peace of God, which transcends all understanding, will guard your hearts and your minds in Christ Jesus. (Philippians 4:6–7 NIV)

Anxiety—the feeling of overwhelming anxiousness or panic—can come in many different forms and produce different outcomes. It can paralyse us and make us fearful of situations that may or may not ever occur. Anxiety can look like nervous energy, unsettled spirits, impatience, and being overly concerned.

Wringing the hands—or just an unsettled heart—can be a sign of anxiety. I'm not sure if Paul ever dealt with anxiety, but he does provide us with a solution for the anxious feelings we may experience throughout life.

He says specifically to not be anxious about anything—our future, our concerns, our habits. Nothing. When anxiety comes, we can do as Paul suggests: pray. And he says to pray with thanksgiving, remembering all we have to be thankful for. Paul's prescription forces our minds off of our concerns and shifts them to our blessings. It's a mind change—an intentional decision to focus on what God has done for us.

Try it. And watch the anxiety flee as you thank God. Watch your list of thanksgiving grow as you rattle off another thing to be grateful for. And like with any good medicine, you can expect relief—in the form of peace. But this is no ordinary peace. It's the peace of God that transcends our understanding.

No, your situation may not change instantly, but you can change and allow peace and gratitude to calm your nerves and shift your focus.

"HELP FOR ANXIETY" FROM *NAVIGATING THE BLUES* BY KATARA WASHINGTON PATTON

_____

_____

_____

_____

_____

_____

_____

_____

_____

_____

_____

_____

_____

_____

Father, I admit my first response to a crisis is often panic, not peace. Thank you for providing a better way through Philippians 4:6–8. Remind me to pray first, reign in my wayward thoughts, and replace them with those that are true, lovely, excellent, and praiseworthy. Help me keep my eyes on you and not my circumstances. Overshadow my heart with peace as I trust in you. In Jesus's name I pray, amen.

FROM *REFRESH YOUR HOPE* BY LORI HATCHER

Letting the Spirit control your mind leads to life and peace.

ROMANS 8:6 NLT

Whenever anything begins to disintegrate your life with Jesus Christ, turn to him at once and ask him to establish rest. Never allow anything that is causing dis-peace to remain. Treat every disturbance as something to wrestle against, not as something to endure.

FROM *MY UTMOST FOR HIS HIGHEST,* MODERN CLASSIC EDITION,

BY OSWALD CHAMBERS

Our friendship with Jesus undergirds our life just as it did for Mary, Martha, and Lazarus. Just as the sisters turned to Jesus for help, so too we can ask God to intervene in our lives, whether we're wrestling over a wayward child or crying out to God to stop injustice or waiting for him to answer our heartfelt pleas. He hears us and will answer according to his mercy and grace.

As we walk day by day with Jesus, sharing our joys and our sorrows, he will meet with us. He'll never leave us to wallow alone but will take our hand in his, giving us peace even as we grieve or rejoice. He'll inspire us to serve him with our gifts and talents, and he'll welcome us to lean on him. What a Friend! What a Savior!

FROM *TRANSFORMING LOVE* BY AMY BOUCHER PYE

I have told you all this so that you may have peace in me.
Here on earth you will have many trials and sorrows. But
take heart, because I have overcome the world.

JOHN 16:33 NLT

_____

_____

_____

_____

_____

_____

_____

_____

_____

_____

_____

_____

_____

_____

Jesus defies all our expectations. The irony of the ages is that this conqueror won peace not with a sword but with a cross, not by killing His enemies but by forgiving them, not by avoiding death but by giving His life for humankind . . . for us.

FROM *40 DAYS. 40 WORDS.* BY KEN PETERSEN & RANDY PETERSEN

Therefore, since we have been justified by faith, we have
peace with God through our Lord Jesus Christ. Through him
we have also obtained access by faith into this grace in which
we stand, and we rejoice in hope of the glory of God.

ROMANS 5:1-2 ESV

I've lived through the scare of my husband's extended unemployment (twice). I've trembled while waiting for biopsy results. I've wept as Satan lured away those I love. I've wailed as death robbed our family of loved ones.

Yet in the depth of every nightmare, God has been there, wrapping me in His warm embrace and whispering truth into my frightened heart.

"It's okay," He's said, drawing me close. "I'm here. You don't have to be afraid."

Through believing friends, timely messages, and His Word, He's spoken truth into my heart. He's comforted me with His promises and banished my fears.

He's sung over me, quieting my trembling heart—leading me to understand at the deepest part of me, *Jesus loves me, this I know, for the Bible tells me so.*

He's spread the blanket of peace over my troubled soul and tucked it tightly under my chin. Holding me close in the darkest nights, He's invited me to rest in His embrace.

And He's told me stories.

"Then I saw 'a new heaven and a new earth,' for the first heaven and the first earth had passed away, and there was no longer any sea" (Revelation 21:1 NIV).

"And I heard a loud voice from the throne saying, 'Look! God's dwelling place is now among the people, and he will dwell with them. They will be his people, and God himself will be with them and be their God. "He will wipe every tear from their eyes. There will be no more death" or mourning or crying or pain, for the old order of things has passed away'" (Revelation 21:3–4 NIV).

Every time I cry out, He comforts me in my nightmare and leaves me with His peace.

My response is simple: *Thank you, Jesus. I love you.*

FROM *REFRESH YOUR HOPE* BY LORI HATCHER

THANK GOD FOR TODAY'S BLESSINGS

-
-
-
-
-
-

Now may the Lord of peace himself give you
peace at all times in every way.

The joy of the LORD is your strength.

NEHEMIAH 8:10 NIV

_____

_____

_____

_____

_____

_____

_____

_____

_____

_____

_____

_____

_____

_____

_____

f we didn't know some saintly people personally, we might be tempted to think that their pleasant and peaceful demeanour means they have nothing o bear. Lift the veil. The fact that the peace and the light and the joy of God are there is proof that the burden is there too.

FROM *MY UTMOST FOR HIS HIGHEST*, MODERN CLASSIC EDITION,

BY OSWALD CHAMBERS

Make every effort to keep the unity of the Spirit through the bond of peace. There is one body and one Spirit, just as you were called to one hope when you were called; one Lord, one faith, one baptism, one God and Father of all, who is over all and through all and in all.

EPHESIANS 4:3-6 NIV

As I hunt for truth and discover God's glorious presence all around me, perhaps others will grow curious about the Source of my peace. As I follow after the clues God leaves in my days, maybe others will notice and begin to read the clues He's leaving for them as well. As I unwrap God's gifts and respond to His leading by adjusting the direction of my life, others just may take notice and begin to wonder what they, too, might find in following Him.

FROM *CHRISTMAS CHANGES EVERYTHING* BY ELISA MORGAN

The wisdom that is from above is first pure, then peaceable,
gentle, willing to yield, full of mercy and good fruits,
without partiality and without hypocrisy. Now the fruit of
righteousness is sown in peace by those who make peace.

JAMES 3:17-18 NKJV

Wait for the LORD; be strong and take heart and wait for the LORD.

PSALM 27:14 NIV

_____

_____

_____

_____

_____

_____

_____

_____

_____

_____

_____

_____

_____

_____

_____

_____

My soul finds peace as I echo David: Wait for the Lord. Be strong. Take heart. And wait for the Lord. Wait, my soul. Wait. Wait for God.

I need to remind myself this again and again—wait for God. Take heart; don't give up; be strong; and wait.

Amen—let it be so.

FROM *TRANSFORMING LOVE* BY AMY BOUCHER PYE

Now may the God of peace himself sanctify you completely, and may your whole spirit and soul and body be kept blameless at the coming of our Lord Jesus Christ. He who calls you is faithful; he will surely do it.

1 THESSALONIANS 5:23-24 ESV

_____

_____

_____

_____

_____

_____

_____

_____

_____

_____

_____

_____

If you stop depending upon yourself and your own effort, you have learned to enter into rest because you start depending on God working in and through you. That is the lost secret of humanity. That is the secret Adam and Eve lost in the garden of Eden. That is the secret Jesus Christ came to restore to us.

When we learn to live by the work of God in us instead of our own work, we experience lives that are peaceful, calm, trusting, and undisturbed by circumstances. We can accomplish great things for God, because God is at work in us. The paradox of this principle is that nothing is more active, effective, and powerful than a life lived in God's rest.

FROM *ADVENTURING THROUGH THE BIBLE*, HOME EDITION

BY RAY C. STEDMAN

And let the peace that comes from Christ rule in your
hearts. For as members of one body you are called
to live in peace. And always be thankful.

COLOSSIANS 3:15 NLT

Grace and peace be yours in abundance
through the knowledge of God and of
Jesus our Lord.

2 PETER 1:2 NIV

SOURCES

All sources used with permission.

Boucher Pye, Amy. *Transforming Love: How Friendship with Jesus Changes Us.* Grand Rapids, MI: Our Daily Bread Publishing, 2023.

Byrd, Sandra. *Dwell: 90 Days at Home with God.* Grand Rapids, MI: Our Daily Bread Publishing, 2023.

Chambers, Oswald. *My Utmost for His Highest.* Modern Classic Edition. Authorized by the Oswald Chambers Publications Association, Ltd. Grand Rapids, MI: Our Daily Bread Publishing, 2023.

Crowder, Bill. *Wisdom for Our Worries: Finding Joy and Peace in Difficult Times.* Grand Rapids, MI: Our Daily Bread Publishing, 2023.

Hatcher, Lori. *Refresh Your Hope: 60 Devotions for Trusting God with All Your Heart.* Grand Rapids, MI: Our Daily Bread Publishing, 2023.

Morgan, Elisa. *Christmas Changes Everything: How the Birth of Jesus Brings Hope to the World.* Grand Rapids, MI: Our Daily Bread Publishing, 2022.

Myra, Harold. *Freedom from My Fears: 40 Meditations on David's Psalms and Prayers.* Grand Rapids, MI: Our Daily Bread Publishing, 2023.

Patton, Katara Washington. *Navigating the Blues: Where to Turn When Worry, Anxiety, or Depression Steals Your Hope.* Grand Rapids, MI: Our Daily Bread Publishing, 2023.

Petersen, Ken, and Randy Petersen. *40 Days. 40 Words. Easter Readings to Touch Your Heart.* Grand Rapids, MI: Our Daily Bread Publishing, 2023.

Smith, Laura L. *Restore My Soul: The Power and Promise of 30 Psalms.* Grand Rapids, MI: Our Daily Bread Publishing, 2022.

Stedman, Ray C. *Adventuring through the Bible: A Guide to the Entire Bible.* Home Edition. Grand Rapids, MI: Our Daily Bread Publishing, 2022.

PERMISSIONS AND CREDITS

For more resources from Our Daily Bread Publishing, visit odb.org/store.